Fact Finders®

Ancient Egyptian Civilization

Mummies
of Ancient Egypt

Revised Edition

by Brianna Hall

Consultant:
Jennifer Houser Wegner, PhD
Associate Curator, Egyptian Section
Penn Museum, Pennsylvania

CAPSTONE PRESS
a capstone imprint

Fact Finder Books are published by Capstone Press,
1710 Roe Crest Drive, North Mankato, Minnesota 56003
www.capstonepub.com

Library of Congress Cataloging-in-Publication Data
Hall, Brianna.
  Mummies of ancient Egypt / by Brianna Hall.
    p. cm. — (Fact finders. Ancient Egyptian civilization)
  Summary: "Describes history of mummies of ancient Egypt"—Provided by publisher.
  Includes bibliographical references and index.
  ISBN 978-1-6690-5116-9 (ebook pdf)
  ISBN 978-1-6690-5117-6 (paperback)
  1. Mummies—Egypt—Juvenile literature. 2. Funeral rites and ceremonies—Egypt—Juvenile
literature. I. Title. II. Series: Fact finders. Ancient Egyptian civilization.
  DT62.M7H34 2012
  932.01—dc23   2011036738

Editorial Credits

Mari Bolte, editor; Juliette Peters, series designer; Svetlana Zhurkin,
    photo researcher; Laura Manthe, production specialist

Photo Credits

Alamy: Dallet-Alba, 18, Danita Delimont, 13, REUTERS, 22, The Art Gallery Collection,
21, The Print Collector, 15; Bridgeman Art Library: Louvre, Paris, France/Christian Larrieu,
9; Getty Images: AFP/PHOTO BRUNO FERRANDEZ, 29, Bettmann, 10, Patrick Landmann,
20, Sergio, 16; Library of Congress: 4; Newscom: AFP/Khaled Desouki, 23, akg-images/Coll. B.
Garrett, 5, akg-images/François Guénet, 6, EPA/Khaled El-Fiqi, 27, EPA/Mike Nelson, 26;
Shutterstock Premier: Gianni Dagli Orti, 11; Shutterstock: artform (hieroglyphs), throughout,
Brian Maudsley, 7, Fedor Selivanov (fact box frame), throughout, Mikhail Dudarev (pyramids),
cover and throughout, Rafa Irusta (papyrus background), throughout, R-studio (background
texture), cover and throughout, Studio 37, cover (front), Zbynek Burival, 25

TABLE OF CONTENTS

Chapter 1

An Amazing Discovery

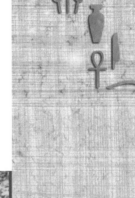

It was a hot day in July 1881 near the Valley of the Kings in Egypt. German **archaeologist** Émile Brugsch lowered himself into a cave. Blinking from the sudden shift to darkness, he saw dozens of shadowy shapes. It only took him a moment to realize he stood in a **tomb** full of mummies.

Coffins were propped against the wall. There were more on the floor, stacked on top of one another. There were also jars, statues, pots, texts, tools, and jewelry.

Brugsch's tomb site, 1902

archaeologist: a scientist who studies how people lived in the past

tomb: a grave, room, or building that holds a dead body

Studying Egyptian mummies became popular in the late 1800s.

Brugsch and his team found 50 mummies and nearly 6,000 objects that day. The find became known as the Deir el Bahri **cache**. Before the discovery, Europeans had only read about the pharaohs. Now they could see mummies up close. A craze for Egyptian culture swept the continent. People couldn't get enough of the gods, **pharaohs**, and mummies of ancient Egypt.

cache: a hidden place where something is stored

pharaoh: a king of ancient Egypt

Chapter 2

Preparing for the Afterlife

The ancient Egyptians believed that everyone was born with a ba and a ka. The ba was the person's character or personality. The ka was the person's life force. When a person died, their ba and ka separated. The ba could go to the **underworld**, but the ka stayed with the person's body. If the person's body was destroyed, their ka would be lost.

Tutankhamun (center) and his ka (right) are greeted by the god Osiris.

underworld: the place where ancient Egyptians believed spirits of the dead go

To the ancient Egyptians, death was simply an interruption before reaching the next stage in life. Going from life to the afterlife was tricky. The ancient Egyptians believed that all parts of the person must be kept whole—body, spirit, and name. They also chanted spells after a person's death. They believed the special words gave the person's ka courage, wit, and strength.

What's in a Name?

The Egyptians believed a person's name was important. If a person died without their name written down, they would not go on to the afterlife. Names were recorded on pieces of **papyrus**, on statues, and on tomb walls. Priests and family members honored the person's name with spells.

The pharaoh Hatshepsut's name carved into stone

papyrus: a material made from a water plant that the ancient Egyptians used like paper

Chapter 3

Making a Mummy

Making a mummy was a long process. A priest called the Overseer of Mysteries was in charge. He directed ceremonies and read chants that protected the dead person's ka.

Priests who performed the **mummification** wore masks. They wanted to look like Anubis, the god of **embalming** and mummification. If the priests did a good job, the mummy would enjoy the afterlife. If not, the person's ka would be lost forever.

After the body was washed with oil and wine, the internal organs were removed. Workers called bandagers cut a hole in the side of the body. Next they removed the internal organs. All the organs, except the heart, were placed in **canopic jars**. Egyptians believed that the mummies would reunite with their organs in the afterlife.

mummification: the process of making a mummy to preserve a dead person's body

embalming: preserving a dead body so it does not decay

canopic jar: a jar in which the ancient Egyptians preserved the organs of a dead person

A Heavy Heart

The ancient Egyptians believed that a person's heart was the key to the afterlife. In death, protective charms were often placed over the mummy's heart.

In the afterlife, gods weighed the dead person's heart on a scale. People who led good lives had hearts that balanced on the scale. They entered paradise. A demon called Amamet ate the hearts of those who tipped the scale. Then the unworthy person entered a world of fire forever.

Each canopic jar was protected by a son of the god Horus. Each god guarded a specific organ.

Duamutef
stomach

Imsety
liver

Qebehsenuef
intestines

Hapy
lungs

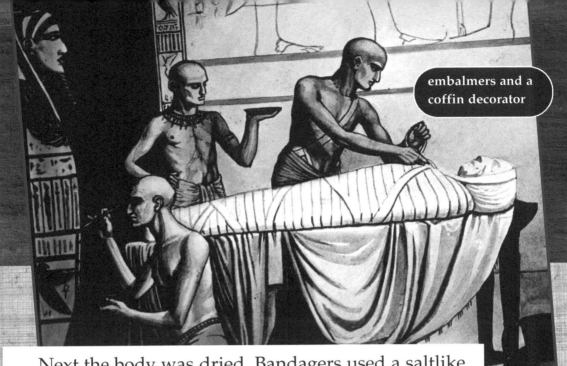

embalmers and a coffin decorator

Next the body was dried. Bandagers used a saltlike substance called natron. The natron was piled up and around the body. Embalmers also filled the inside of the body with natron. Over the next 40 days, the body lost 75 percent of its original weight. Another 30 days were spent wrapping the mummy in bandages.

Workers stuffed the mummy with packing material, such as rags or sawdust. The stuffing helped the body look more full and lifelike. Spices and oils, such as cinnamon and myrrh, made the body smell nice. A coat of resin or beeswax kept pests away.

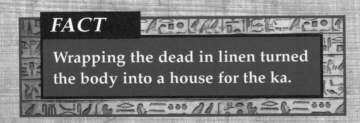

FACT

Wrapping the dead in linen turned the body into a house for the ka.

Small charms called **amulets** were placed in the mummy's wrappings and around the body. These charms protected both the living and the dead.

The shapes and colors of each amulet were important. Green or blue amulets symbolized rebirth. Red stood for energy or power. Popular shapes included animals, symbols based on **hieroglyphs**, or gods.

Small statues, called shabtis, were often included at burial sites. These figures would help the dead person in the afterlife. They were there to do unpleasant work, such as farming or building things. Most tombs contained between one and 10 shabtis. Some tombs had a shabti for every day of the year.

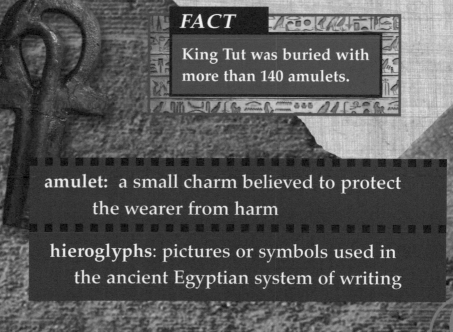

FACT

King Tut was buried with more than 140 amulets.

amulet: a small charm believed to protect the wearer from harm

hieroglyphs: pictures or symbols used in the ancient Egyptian system of writing

Mummies were placed inside coffins for burial. Early coffins were very plain. Around the end of the Old Kingdom (2625–2130 BC), the inside of the coffin was decorated with words. These writings were called Coffin Texts. Egyptians believed that these spells would help the dead pass into the afterlife safely.

Rich Egyptians hired artists to decorate their coffins with golden paint, pictures, and protective spells. Some coffins were painted with maps of the underworld. The map would ensure the person's spirit would not get lost. Others were painted with protective symbols, such as eyes, wings, or gods. Poor people bought simple, premade coffins.

Mummies of the richest Egyptians were placed inside several coffins. Sometimes the coffins were human-shaped and decorated with gold paint, colored glass, and hieroglyphs. Coffins of pharaohs and other important people were placed inside a large stone case called a **sarcophagus**.

sarcophagus: a stone coffin

FACT

Today's scholars disagree about the order of pharaohs and family kingdoms and dynasties. Over time, the keeping of records became disorganized. Some records have been lost.

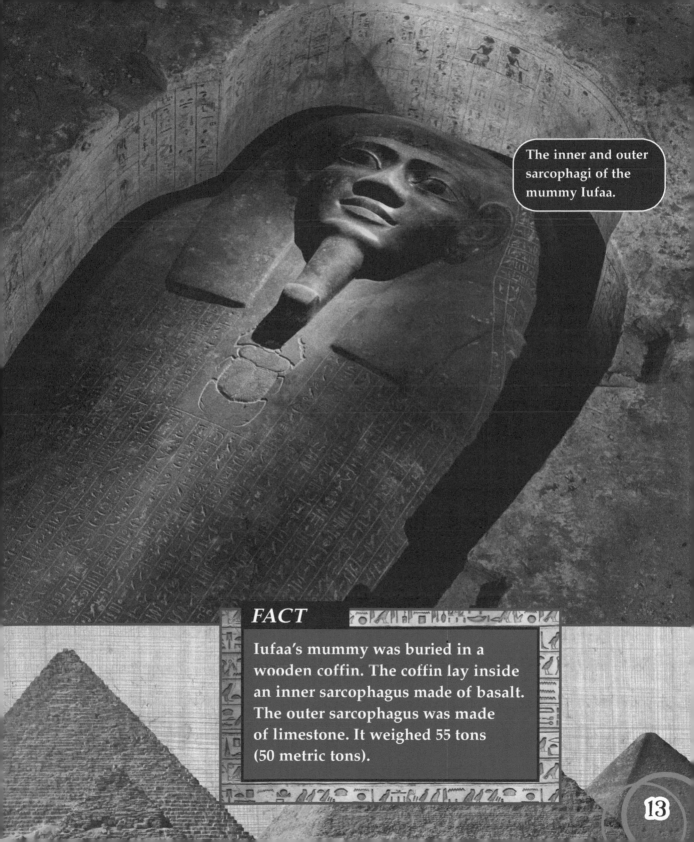

The inner and outer sarcophagi of the mummy Iufaa.

FACT

Iufaa's mummy was buried in a wooden coffin. The coffin lay inside an inner sarcophagus made of basalt. The outer sarcophagus was made of limestone. It weighed 55 tons (50 metric tons).

Tombs and Pyramids

Most mummies were buried in tombs. These "houses of eternity" had two parts. An underground chamber held the coffin and the mummy's burial goods. An offering place chapel was above ground. There, the living asked the dead for help or advice. They wrote their wishes on scrolls so the dead could read them.

The tomb and chapel could be simple or complex, depending on the person's importance. Pharaohs and wealthy people built tombs of quarried stone. These huge tombs were expensive and took years to finish. Poorer people sometimes made small tombs of mudbrick. Other times they buried coffins directly in the sand.

Tombs became bigger and more complicated around 2700 BC. Pharaoh Djoser wished to demonstrate his power and wealth. He built Egypt's first pyramid tomb, the Step Pyramid, near Cairo. The Step Pyramid still stands today. It has six tiers and is around 200 feet (61 meters) high.

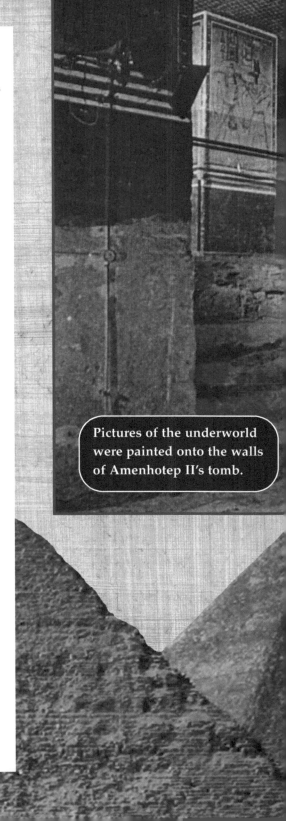

Pictures of the underworld were painted onto the walls of Amenhotep II's tomb.

Less than a hundred years later, Pharaoh Khufu built the Great Pyramid of Giza. This huge tomb is made up of more than 2.3 million blocks of limestone. It weighs an estimated 7 million tons (6.4 metric tons).

Djoser, Khufu, and other pharaohs wanted to continue enjoying the luxuries they experienced on Earth. They believed large and beautiful tombs would help them maintain their royal status in the afterlife.

Chapter 4

Burials

With the body prepared and the tombs built, the mummy could be put to rest. Priests and family members walked to the burial site. Wealthier people hired professional mourners. The mourners cried and beat their chests with grief.

Women performed a ceremonial dance at the burial site. Things such as furniture, weapons, jewelry, and the canopic jars were placed in the tomb. Food was brought for the mummy to eat in the afterlife.

The Path to the Afterlife

Ancient Egyptians believed the path to the afterlife was full of dangers, such as monsters and riddles. To help the spirits, priests wrote a sort of guide to the underworld. The collection of spells was known as the *Book of the Dead*.

These scrolls were very expensive. Scribes wrote every word by hand on papyrus. Wealthy Egyptians could afford their own copy of the text. These scrolls were buried with the mummies. Poor people had phrases from the text carved onto their coffin or simply spoken before burial.

Before the mummy could be buried, a **ritual** called the Opening of the Mouth took place. The ceremony had more than 75 steps and was performed by an official called a sem-priest. The sem-priest touched an adze, a type of carpenter's tool, to the mummy's face. This process would help the mummy see, speak, eat, and move in the afterlife.

After the ceremony, a final prayer was said. Then the mummy was buried. Mourners then took part in a feast near the tomb.

ritual: an action that is always done the same way

Chapter 5

Famous Mummies

For years, pharaohs were buried in pyramids located in northern Egypt. Many were buried near the Giza Plateau. However, during the New Kingdom (1539–1075 BC), the pharaohs moved south to the Valley of the Kings. More than 60 tombs of New Kingdom rulers are located in the valley.

The tomb of Seti I in the Valley of the Kings

It Took How Long?

Building a tomb was a long process that could take a lifetime to complete. Hundreds of builders, artists, and scribes were needed. During the New Kingdom, workers and their families lived near the Valley of the Kings. They were the only people who knew the location of the valley, also called the Place of Truth. Secrecy helped protect the tombs from grave robbers.

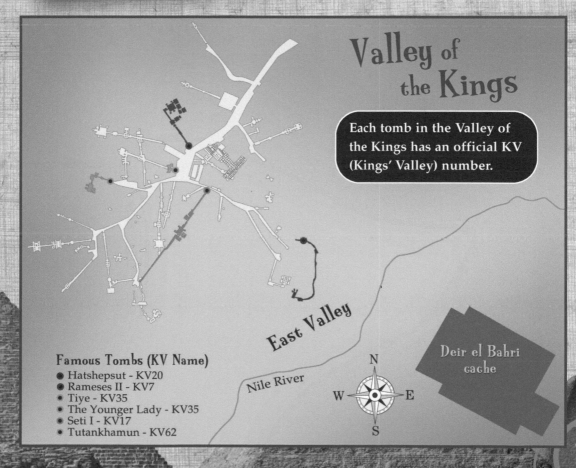

Valley of the Kings

Each tomb in the Valley of the Kings has an official KV (Kings' Valley) number.

East Valley

Deir el Bahri cache

Nile River

N
W   E
S

Famous Tombs (KV Name)
- Hatshepsut - KV20
- Rameses II - KV7
- Tiye - KV35
- The Younger Lady - KV35
- Seti I - KV17
- Tutankhamun - KV62

Rule: 1294 or 1290–1279 BC
Discovered: 1881
Original Tomb Location:
Valley of the Kings (KV17)
Tomb Uncovered:
Deir el Bahri cache

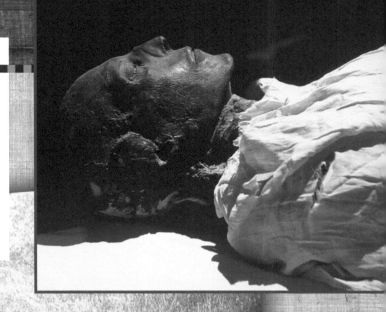

Seti I was a successful and respected pharaoh. But his reign was a short one. He began many building projects that were not completed in his lifetime.

Seti planned a long, deep tomb in the Valley of the Kings. It was cut into hundreds of feet of rock. A well was built into the tomb to keep flood waters from ruining the tomb. It would also trap careless grave robbers.

The tomb was beautifully decorated with detailed scenes and writings. Religious texts and magical spells lined the walls and pillars of the tombs. Large paintings showed scenes of the gods and the underworld. His sarcophagus was covered with hieroglyphs and carvings.

When the tomb was first explored in 1817, archaeologists noticed that Seti's mummy was missing. Decades later, the pharaoh's mummy was found at the royal cache in Deir el Bahri. Priests likely moved the mummy to protect it from grave robbers.

Pharaoh Rameses II

Rule: 1279–1212 BC
Discovered: 1881
Original Tomb Location:
Valley of the Kings (KV7)
Tomb Uncovered:
Deir el Bahri cache

Also known as Rameses the Great, the son of Seti I ruled for 66 years. He was one of the longest-reigning pharaohs. He was also one of the oldest, living until 92. He had eight wives and at least 100 children. His large family gave him the nickname The Great Ancestor.

Rameses was originally buried in the Valley of the Kings. His tomb spans more than 8,800 square feet (818 square meters). It is one of the largest in the valley. His temple, called the Ramesseum, is also large, at 984 feet (300 m) long and 640 feet (195 m) wide.

Unfortunately, the tomb has not stood the test of time. Flood waters ruined wall paintings. Thieves also broke into his tomb and stole valuables. Priests moved his mummy to keep it safe. It was first moved in 1054 BC, to Seti I's resting place. It was later moved again to the Deir el Bahri cache.

Queen Tiye, the "Elder Lady"

Queen: 1389–1338 BC
Discovered: 1898
Original Tomb Location:
Valley of the Kings (KV35)

Queen Tiye married the pharaoh Amenhotep III at a very young age. She was beloved by her husband. The two were often shown together in paintings and statues. She helped Amenhotep make decisions in court about war and trade. Her face was carved onto a sphinx statue, an honor usually only for pharaohs. After her husband died, Tiye acted as an adviser for her son, Akhenaten.

Archaeologists found Tiye's mummy in a tomb with more than a dozen other royals. Her body was unwrapped and unmarked. Some believe the mummies were moved to protect them from grave robbers.

For a century, scholars called this unknown mummy the "Elder Lady." They guessed her identity after some of her long, red hair was found in Tutankhamun's tomb. The hair was in a small coffin marked with her name.

In 2010 DNA tests proved that the mummy was Tiye. Scientists had already taken the DNA of Tiye's parents, Yuya and Tuyu. After taking the Elder Lady's DNA, they were finally able to identify the lost queen.

The "Younger Lady"

Lived: circa 1340 BC
Discovered: 1898
Original Tomb Location:
Valley of the Kings (KV35)

Her name is unknown, and her story is full of mystery. This mummy was found alongside the Elder Lady. Scientists named her the "Younger Lady."

For years historians debated who the mummy could have been. For a long time, people thought she was either Queen Nefertiti or Princess Kiya. Both were wives of Pharaoh Akhenaten. In 2010 scientists took DNA from a number of mummies. They were shocked at what they learned. The Younger Lady was one of pharaoh Akhenaten's five known sisters. She was also the mother of his son, Tutankhamun.

FACT
Ancient Egyptians believed that gods could only marry other gods. Sometimes this meant they married their siblings. Because pharaohs were seen as earthly gods, this practice was common among Egyptian royal families too.

How Were They Connected?

In 2010 scientists took DNA samples from 11 mummies. They looked at the mummies' genetic markers to figure out family lines. Certain markers are passed from parents to children. Scientists compared these markers with already-established information, such as ruling periods and tomb writings. They were able to draw a family tree that started with Yuya and Tuyu and ended with Tutankhamun.

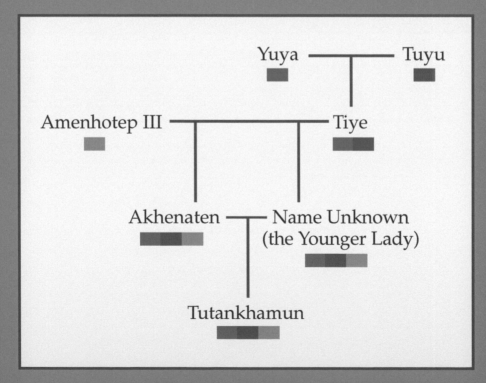

Pharaoh Tutankhamun

Rule: 1333–1323 BC
Discovered: 1922
Original Tomb Location:
Valley of the Kings (KV62)

Pharaoh Tutankhamun is the most well-known Egyptian ruler. He became pharaoh when he was 9 years old. He died 10 years later.

King Tut is not famous for his rule or his lifestyle. He is famous because of his tomb. His small tomb in the Valley of the Kings remained untouched for more than 3,000 years. Howard Carter uncovered the tomb in 1922. He found more than 5,000 artifacts. The discovery fascinated the world.

It took 10 years to remove, clean, and document all of the objects. Today Tut's mummy still rests in the Valley of the Kings. Instead of resting in its gold sarcophagus, it now sleeps in a climate-controlled container. This glass box keeps the mummy from further damage.

FACT

Tut's golden burial mask stands nearly 2 feet (0.6 m) tall. It is decorated with gold, glass, and precious stones.

Pharaoh Hatshepsut

Rule: 1479–1457 BC
Discovered: 1903
Original Tomb Location:
Valley of the Kings (KV20)
Tomb Uncovered:
Valley of the Kings

Pharaoh Hatshepsut was the longest reigning female pharaoh. She was also one of the few female leaders. She built complex temples and statues for the royal family and the gods. Even though she was a woman, statues and paintings show her wearing the symbols of a male pharaoh, such as a false beard or a man's crown and clothing. Some writings even refer to her as "he" or "him."

Hatshepsut had a tomb 656 feet (200 m) long in the Valley of the Kings. However, when the tomb was discovered in 1903, there were no mummies to be found. The sarcophagus inside was empty and unused.

Later, the tomb of Hatshepsut's nurse was found nearby. There were two female mummies inside. Scientists thought one might be Hatshepsut. But because there was no way to identify the body, they left it in the tomb. The mummy was finally removed and positively identified as Hatshepsut in 2007.

Other Mummies

Animal Mummies

Millions of animal mummies dating back to ancient Egypt lay buried in the sands. Crocodiles, birds, baboons, and cats were the most common animals made into mummies.

Some animal mummies were made to become food sources in the afterlife. Others were meant to be pets.

The people of Ancient Egypt believed that certain animals could represent certain gods. In the early days of Egyptian civilization, each town was represented by an animal. These animals were much like team mascots today. When a person became pharaoh, their town animal was given the status of a god.

Portrait Mummies

Romans took control of Egypt in 30 BC. This change in rule also changed mummy making. Less time was spent preserving the body and more time was spent decorating it. Mummies were wrapped in criss-cross patterns. Lifelike portraits were painted on wood and placed over the mummy's face. The faces were lifelike and did not contain religious symbols. Portrait mummies were some of the last mummies made in Egypt.

Chapter 6

Mummies Today

By studying mummies, scientists can learn more about how ancient Egyptians lived. A hundred years ago, people learned about mummies by unwrapping them. After the mummies were taken apart and studied, they were usually thrown out.

Wild Mummy Uses

Would you go to a mummy unwrapping party? The first party of this type took place in the 1500s. However, they did not become popular until the 1900s. Rich men would buy mummies in secret and invite their friends over. Unwrapping a mummy was a frightening and unique form of entertainment.

Once the fun was over, the wrappings and body parts were sold or thrown out. Peddlers would crush the dusty linens and dry mummies into medicine. They claimed the powder had healing powers.

Today scientists and historians use X-ray machines, scans, and chemical analysis to study mummies. Studying mummies closely teaches them how ancient Egyptians worked, what they ate, and how they died.

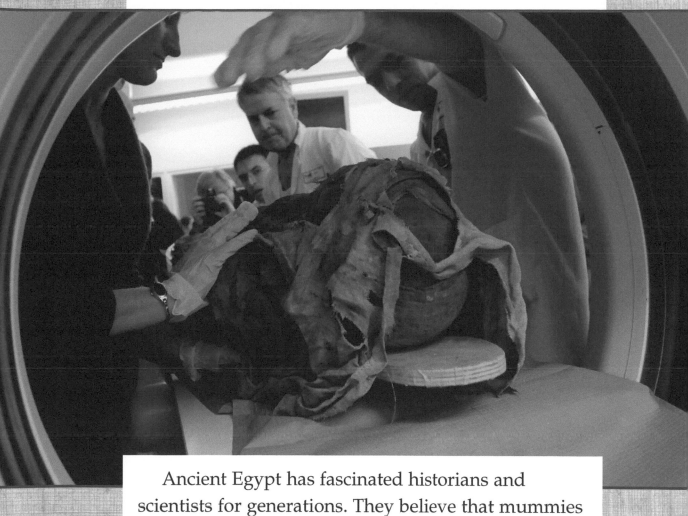

Ancient Egypt has fascinated historians and scientists for generations. They believe that mummies provide a window to the past civilization. Scientists continue to unwrap the mystery of the mummy. As more mummies are discovered, researchers will continue to uncover the secrets of the ancient world.

GLOSSARY

amulet (AM-yoo-let)—a small charm believed to protect the wearer from harm

archaeologist (ar-kee-OL-uh-jist)—a scientist who studies how people lived in the past

cache (KASH)—a hidden place where something is stored

canopic jar (kuh-NO-pik JAR)—a jar in which the ancient Egyptians preserved the organs of a dead person

embalming (im-BALM-ing)—preserving a dead body so it does not decay

hieroglyphs (HYE-ruh-glif)—pictures or symbols used in the ancient Egyptian system of writing

mummification (muh-mi-fuh-KAY-shun)—the process of making a mummy to preserve a dead person's body

papyrus (puh-PYE-ruhss)—a tall water plant that grows in northern Africa and southern Europe; a material that is written on can be made from the stems of this plant.

pharaoh (FAIR-oh)—a king of ancient Egypt

ritual (RICH-oo-uhl)—an action that is always done the same way

sarcophagus (sar-KAH-fuh-guhs)—a stone coffin; the ancient Egyptians placed inner coffins into a sarcophagus

tomb (TOOM)—a grave, room, or building that holds a dead body

underworld (UHN-dur-wurld)—the place under the earth where ancient Egyptians believed spirits of the dead go

Biskup, Agnieszka. *Egypt's Mysterious Pyramids: An Isobel Soto Archaeology Adventure.* Graphic Expeditions. Mankato, Minn.: Capstone Press, 2012.

Knapp, Ron. *Mummy Secrets Uncovered.* Bizarre Science. Berkeley Heights, N.J.: Enslow Publishers, 2011.

Malam, John. *100 Things You Should Know about Mummies.* Broomall, Penn.: Mason Crest Publishers, 2011.

INTERNET SITES

FactHound offers a safe, fun way to find Internet sites related to this book. All of the sites on FactHound have been researched by our staff.

Here's all you do:

Visit *www.facthound.com*

Type in this code: 9781429676298

Super-cool stuff!

Check out projects, games and lots more at
www.capstonekids.com

INDEX